Sunny Day Dresses for Babies & Toddlers

Lime Green A-Line Dress
Page 2

Vanilla Baby Dress
Page 10

**Orange Baby Dress
with Collar**
Page 6

Lime Green A-Line Dress

Skill Level

⬛⬛⬛⬜ INTERMEDIATE

Finished Sizes

Instructions given fit size 12 months; changes for sizes 2, 3 and 4 are in [ ].

Materials

- Royale Silkessence Microfiber fine (sport) weight yarn (2 oz/124 yds/56g per ball):
    4 [4, 5, 6] balls #2236 lt. yellow green (lime)
    1 ball #2101 white
- Sizes D/3/3.25mm and H/8/5mm crochet hooks or size needed to obtain gauge
- Tapestry needle

Gauge

With H hook: [Cl, ch 1] 9 times = 4½ inches; 14 pattern rows = 4 inches

Pattern Notes

Weave in ends as work progresses.

Chain-2 at beginning of half double crochet row counts as first half double crochet unless otherwise stated.

Chain-3 at beginning of double crochet row counts as first double crochet unless otherwise stated.

Special Stitches

Cluster (cl): Insert hook in indicated st, yo, draw lp through, [insert hook in next st, yo, draw lp through] twice, yo and draw through all 4 lps on hook.

Small cluster (small cl): Insert hook in indicated st, yo, draw lp through, insert hook in next st, yo, draw lp through, yo and draw through all 3 lps on hook.

Instructions

Front
First Shoulder

Row 1 (WS): With H hook and lime, ch 6, sc in 2nd ch from hook, sc in each ch across, turn. *(5 sc)*

Row 2 (RS): Ch 1, sc in first sc, **cl** *(see Special Stitches)* in last sc and in next 2 sc, ch 1, cl in last sc and in next 2 sc, (sc, hdc) in same sc as last leg of last cl worked, turn. *(2 sc, 2 cls, 1 ch st, 1 hdc)*

Row 3: Ch 2 *(see Pattern Notes)*, **small cl** *(see Special Stitches)* in first hdc and in next sc, [ch 1, cl in same sc and in next 2 sts] twice, sc in same st as last leg of last cl made, turn. *(1 hdc, 1 small cl, 2 cls, 2 ch sts, 1 sc)*

Note: On rem rows, cl is worked in same st as last st made and in next 2 sts.

Row 4: Ch 1, sc in first sc, [cl, ch 1] twice, cl, (sc, hdc) in same st as last leg of last cl made, fasten off. *(1 hdc, 3 cls, 2 ch sts, 2 sc)*

2nd Shoulder

Row 1 (WS): With H hook and lime, ch 6, sc in 2nd ch from hook, sc in each ch across, turn. *(5 sc)*

Row 2 (RS): Ch 2 *(see Pattern Notes)*, sc in first sc, cl, ch 1, cl, sc in same st as last leg of last cl made, turn. *(2 sc, 2 cls, 1 ch st, 1 hdc)*

Row 3: Ch 1, sc in first sc, [cl, ch 1] twice, small cl in same st as last leg of last cl made and in 2nd ch of beg ch-2, hdc in same ch as last leg of last small cl made, turn. *(1 sc, 2 cls, 1 small cl, 1 hdc, 2 ch sts)*

Row 4: Ch 2, sc in first st, [cl, ch 1] twice, cl, sc in same st as last leg of last cl made, turn. *(1 hdc, 2 sc, 3 cls, 2 ch sts)*

Body

Row 5: Ch 1, sc in first st, [cl, ch 1] 3 times, small cl in same st as last leg of last cl made and in 2nd ch of beg ch-2, hdc in same ch as last leg of last small cl made, ch 21 [21, 23, 25], hold First Shoulder with WS facing, hdc in first hdc on First Shoulder, small cl in same st and in next st, ch 1, cl, [ch 1, cl] twice, hdc in same st as last leg of last cl made, turn. *(1 sc, 3 hdc, 6 cls, 27 [27, 29, 31] ch sts)*

Row 6: Ch 1, sc in first st, cl, *ch 1, cl, rep from * across, sc in same st as last leg of last cl made, turn. *(2 sc, 19 [19, 20, 21] cls, 18 [18, 19, 20] ch sts)*

Rows 7–16 [7–18, 7–20, 7–22]: Rep row 6.

Rows 17 & 18 [19 & 20, 21 & 22, 23 & 24]: Ch 3 *(see Pattern Notes)*, (hdc, sc) in first st, cl, *ch 1, cl, rep from * across, (sc, hdc, dc)

in same st as last leg of last cl worked, turn. *(2 sc, 4 hdc, 4 dc, 21 [21, 22, 23] cls, 20 [20, 21, 22] ch sts at end of last row)*

Rows 19–23 [21–25, 23–27, 25–29]: Rep row 6.

Row 24 [26, 28, 30]: Ch 1, 2 sc in first st, cl, *ch 1, cl, rep from * across, 2 sc in same st as last leg of last cl made, turn. *(4 sc, 23 [23, 24, 25] cls, 22 [22, 23, 24] ch sts)*

Row 25 [27, 29, 31]: Ch 1, 2 sc in first st, sc in next st, cl, *ch 1, cl, rep from * across to last st, sc in same st as last leg of last cl made, 2 sc in last st, turn. *(6 sc, 23 [23, 24, 25] cls, 22 [22, 23, 24] ch sts)*

Rows 26–31 [28–33, 30–35, 32–37]: Rep row 6.

Rows 32 & 33 [34 & 35, 36 & 37, 38 & 39]: Rep rows 24 and 25 [26 and 27, 28 and 29, 30 and 31]. *(6 sc, 25 [25, 28, 29] cls, 24 [24, 27, 28] ch sts at end of last row)*

Rows 34–39 [36–41, 38–43, 40–45]: Rep row 6.

Rows 40 & 41 [42 & 43, 44 & 45, 46 & 47]: Rep rows 24 and 25 [26 and 27, 28 and 29, 30 and 31]. *(6 sc, 27 [27, 30, 31] cls, 25 [25, 29, 30] ch sts at end of last row)*

Rows 42–47 [44–49, 46–51, 48–53]: Rep row 6.

Rows 48 & 49 [50 & 51, 52 & 53, 54 & 55]: Rep rows 24 and 25 [26 and 27, 28 and 29, 30 and 31]. *(6 sc, 29 [29, 32, 33] cls, 28 [28, 31, 32] ch sts at end of last row)*

Rows 50–55 [52–57, 54–59, 56–61]: Rep row 6.

Rows 56 & 57 [58 & 59, 60 & 61, 62 & 63]: Rep rows 24 and 25 [26 and 27, 28 and 29, 30 and 31]. *(6 sc, 31 [31, 34, 35] cls, 30 [30, 33, 34] ch sts at end of last row)*

Rows 58 & 59 [60 & 61, 62 & 63, 64 & 65]: Rep row 6. At end of last row, **do not turn**.

Edging

Ch 1, working across next side in ends of rows, sc in each row across to row 19 [21, 23, 25], fasten off.

Hold Front with RS facing and unworked side at top, with H hook, join lime in end of row 19 [21, 23, 25], ch 1, sc in end of same row, sc in each row across, fasten off.

Back
First Shoulder

Row 1 (WS): With H hook and lime, ch 6, sc in 2nd ch from hook, sc in each ch across, turn. *(5 sc)*

Row 2 (RS): Ch 1, sc in first sc, **cl** *(see Special Stitches)* in last sc and in next 2 sc, ch 1, cl, (sc, hdc) in same sc as last leg of last cl worked, turn. *(2 sc, 2 cls, 1 ch st, 1 hdc)*

Row 3: Ch 2 *(see Pattern Notes)*, **small cl** *(see Special Stitches)* in first hdc and in next sc, [ch 1, cl] twice, sc in same st as last leg of last cl made, turn. *(1 hdc, 1 small cl, 2 cls, 2 ch sts, 1 sc)*

Row 4: Ch 1, sc in first sc, [cl, ch 1] twice, cl, (sc, hdc) in same st as last leg of last cl made. *(2 sc, 1 hdc, 3 cls, 2 ch sts, 1 sc)*

Row 5: Ch 2, small cl in first hdc and in next st, [ch 1, cl] 3 times, sc in same st as last leg of last cl made, turn. *(1 sc, 1 hdc, 1 small cl, 3 cls, 3 ch sts, 1 sc)*

Row 6: Ch 1, sc in first st, [cl, ch 1] 4 times, (sc, hdc) in same st as last leg of last cl made, turn. *(4 cls, 3 ch sts, 2 sc, 1 hdc)*

Row 7: Ch 2, sc in first st, cl, [ch 1, cl] 4 times, sc in same st as last leg of last cl made, turn. *(5 cls, 4 ch sts, 2 sc, 1 hdc)*

Row 8: Ch 1, sc in first st, *cl, ch 1, rep from * to last 2 sts, small cl, ch 1, (sc, hdc) in last st, turn. *(5 cls, 4 ch sts, 2 sc)*

Row 9: Ch 2, sc in first st, cl, *ch 1, cl, rep from * across, sc in same st as last leg of last cl made, turn. *(1 hdc, 7 cls, 6 ch sts, 2 sc)*

Row 10: Ch 1, sc in first st, *cl, ch 1, rep from * across to last st, small cl, hdc in last st worked in, turn. *(1 hdc, 1 small cl, 7 cls, 7 ch sts, 1 sc)*

Row 11: Rep row 9. *(1 hdc, 2 sc, 8 cls, 7 ch sts)*

Row 12: Rep row 10. *(1 hdc, 1 small cl, 1 sc, 8 cls, 7 ch sts)*

Row 13: Rep row 9. *(1 hdc, 2 sc, 9 cls, 8 ch sts)*

For Size 12 Months Only

Row 14: Rep row 10. At end of row, fasten off. *(1 hdc, 1 small cl, 1 sc, 9 cls, 9 ch sts)*

For Size 2 Only

Row 14: Rep row 10. *(1 hdc, 1 small cl, 1 sc, 9 cls, 9 ch sts)*

Row 15: Rep row 9. *(1 hdc, 2 sc, 10 cls, 9 ch sts)*

Row 16: Rep row 10. At end of row, fasten off. *(1 hdc, 1 small cl, 1 sc, 10 cls, 10 ch sts)*

For Size 3 Only

Row 14: Rep row 10. *(1 hdc, 1 small cl, 1 sc, 9 cls, 9 ch sts at end of row)*

Row 15: Rep row 9. *(1 hdc, 2 sc, 10 cls, 9 ch sts)*

Row 16: Rep row 10. *(1 hdc, 1 small cl, 1 sc, 10 cls, 10 ch sts)*

Row 17: Rep row 9. *(1 hdc, 2 sc, 11 cls, 10 ch sts)*

Row 18: Rep row 10. At end of row, fasten off. *(1 hdc, 1 small cl, 1 sc, 11 cls, 11 ch sts)*

For Size 4 Only

Row 14: Rep row 10. *(1 hdc, 1 small cl, 1 sc, 9 cls, 9 ch sts at end of row)*

Row 15: Rep row 9. *(1 hdc, 2 sc, 10 cls, 9 ch sts)*

Row 16: Rep row 10. *(1 hdc, 1 small cl, 1 sc, 10 cls, 10 ch sts)*

Row 17: Rep row 9. *(1 hdc, 2 sc, 11 cls, 10 ch sts)*

Row 18: Rep row 10. *(1 hdc, 1 small cl, 1 sc, 11 cls, 11 ch sts)*

Row 19: Rep row 9. *(1 hdc, 2 sc, 12 cls, 11 ch sts)*

Row 20: Rep row 10. At end of row, fasten off. *(1 hdc, 1 small cl, 1 sc, 12 cls, 12 ch sts)*

2nd Shoulder
For All Sizes

Row 1 (WS): With H hook and lime, ch 6, sc in 2nd ch from hook, sc in each ch across, turn. *(5 sc)*

Row 2 (RS): Ch 2, sc in first sc, cl, ch 1, cl, sc in same st as last leg of cl made, turn. *(2 sc, 2 cls, 1 ch st, 1 hdc)*

Row 3: Ch 1, sc in first sc, *cl, ch 1, rep from * across to last st, small cl, hdc in same st as last leg of last small cl made, turn.

Row 4: Ch 2, sc in first st, *cl, ch 1, rep from * across, sc in same st as last leg of last cl made, turn.

Row 5: Ch 1, sc in first st, *cl, ch 1, rep from * across to last st, small cl, hdc in same st as last leg of last small cl made, turn. *(3 cls, 1 small cl, 1 sc, 1 hdc)*

Row 6: Ch 2, sc in first st, *cl, ch 1, cl, rep from * across, sc in same st as last leg of last cl made, turn.

Row 7: Ch 1, sc in first st, *cl, ch 1, rep from * across to last 2 sts, cl, (sc, hdc) same st as last leg of last cl made, turn.

Row 8: Ch 2, sc in first st, ch 1, small cl, *ch 1, cl, rep from * across to last sc, sc in same st as last leg of last cl made, turn. *(1 small cl, 5 cls, 4 ch sts, 1 hdc, 2 sc)*

Row 9: Rep row 7. *(1 hdc, 7 cls, 6 ch sts, 2 sc)*

Row 10: Ch 2, small cl, *ch 1, cl, rep from * across to last st, sc in same st as last leg of last cl made, turn. *(1 hdc, 1 small cl, 7 cls, 6 ch sts, 2 sc)*

Row 11: Ch 2, sc in first st, cl, *ch 1, cl, rep from * across to last st, sc in same st as last leg of last cl made, turn. *(8 cls, 7 ch sts, 2 sc, 1 hdc)*

Row 12: Ch 2, small cl, *ch 1, cl, rep from * across to last st, sc in same st as last leg of last cl made, turn. *(1 hdc, 1 small cl, 8 cls, 8 ch sts, 1 sc)*

Row 13: Ch 1, sc in first st, *cl, ch 1, rep from * across to last st, (sc, hdc) in same st as last leg of last cl made, turn. *(1 hdc, 2 sc, 9 cls, 8 ch sts)*

Row 14: Ch 1, sc in first st, *cl, ch 1, rep from * across to last st, small cl, hdc in last st worked in, turn.

For Size 2 Only

Row 15: Rep row 7. *(1 hdc, 2 sc, 10 cls, 9 ch sts)*

Row 16: Rep row 10. *(1 hdc, 1 sc, 10 cls, 10 ch sts, 1 small cl)*

For Size 3 Only

Row 15: Rep row 7. *(1 hdc, 2 sc, 10 cls, 9 ch sts)*

Row 16: Rep row 10. *(1 hdc, 1 sc, 10 cls, 10 ch sts, 1 small cl)*

Row 17: Rep row 7. *(1 hdc, 1 sc, 11 cls, 10 ch sts)*

Row 18: Rep row 10. *(1 hdc, 1 sc, 11 cls, 11 ch sts, 1 small cl)*

For Size 4 Only

Row 15: Rep row 7. *(1 hdc, 2 sc, 10 cls, 9 ch sts)*

Row 16: Rep row 10. *(1 hdc, 1 sc, 10 cls, 10 ch sts, 1 small cl)*

Row 17: Rep row 7. *(1 hdc, 1 sc, 11 cls, 10 ch sts)*

Row 18: Rep row 10. *(1 hdc, 1 sc, 11 cls, 11 ch sts, 1 small cl)*

Row 19: Rep row 7. *(1 hdc, 2 sc, 12 cls, 11 ch sts)*

Row 20: Rep row 10. *(1 hdc, 1 sc, 12 cls, 12 ch sts, 1 small cl)*

For All Sizes

Row 15 [17, 19, 21]: Ch 1, sc in first st, cl, *ch 1, cl, rep from * across, hold WS of First Shoulder facing, cl in first 3 sts on last row, **ch 1, cl, rep from ** across to last st, sc in same st as last leg of last cl made, turn.

Row 16 [18, 20, 22]: Ch 1, sc in first st, cl, *ch 1, cl, rep from * across, sc in same st as last leg of last cl made, turn.

Rows 17–59 [19–61, 21–63, 23–65]: Rep rows 17–59 [19–61, 21–63, 23–65] of Front Body.

Edging

Work same as Edging for Front Body.

Assembly

Sew Side and Shoulder seams.

Bottom Trim

Rnd 1: Hold piece with RS facing and bottom edge at top, with H hook, join lime in 1 side seam, ch 1, sc same sp, sc in each st around and in other side seam, join in beg sc.

Rnd 2: Ch 5 *(counts as a dc, ch-2 sp)*, dc in same sc, (dc, ch 2, dc) in each sc around, join in 3rd ch of beg ch-5, fasten off.

Top Trim

With H hook, join lime in 1 shoulder seam at neck edge, working from left to right, work **reverse sc** *(see illustration)* in each st around, join in beg reverse sc, fasten off.

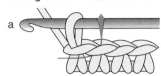

Reverse Single Crochet

Armhole Trim

With H hook, join lime in 1 underarm seam, working from left to right, work reverse sc in each st around, join in beg reverse sc, fasten off.
Rep on other armhole.

Flower Trim
First Flower

With D hook and white, make loose slip knot, leaving a 6-inch end at beg, [ch 2, 2 dc, ch 2, sl st] 5 times in slip knot, tighten knot, fasten off, leaving 6-inch end for sewing.

Remaining Flowers

Make number needed to fit around neckline.

With D hook and white, make loose slip knot, leaving a 6-inch end at beg, [ch 2, 2 dc, ch 2, sl st] 4 times in slip knot, ch 2, 2 dc in slip knot, sk 1 petal on last flower, sl st in 2nd dc of next petal on last flower, ch 2, sl st in knot of present flower, fasten off.

Finishing

Sew Flowers around neck opening with single petal at neck edge. ■

Orange Baby Dress with Collar

Skill Level

 INTERMEDIATE

Finished Sizes

Instructions given fit size 12 months; changes for sizes 2, 3 and 4 are in [ ].

Materials

- Fine (sport) weight yarn: 8 [9, 10, 12] oz/720-800 [810-900, 900-1000, 1080-1200] yds/227 [255, 284, 340]g orange
- Size G/6/4.5mm crochet hook or size needed to obtain gauge
- Tapestry needle
- Sewing needle
- ½-inch shank buttons: 5
- 2 hook and eye closures (optional)
- Matching thread

Gauge

In pattern: [Sc in next st, dc in next st] 9 times = 4 inches; 16 pattern rows = 4 inches

Pattern Notes

Weave in ends as work progresses. Chain-3 at beginning of double crochet row counts as first double crochet unless otherwise stated.

Special Stitch

Shell: (Dc, ch 1, dc, ch 1, dc, ch 1, dc, ch 1, dc) in indicated st.

Instructions

Front
Left Shoulder

Row 1 (WS): Ch 11, sc in 2nd ch from hook, dc in next ch, (sc in next ch, dc in next ch) across, turn. *(5 sc, 5 dc)*

Rows 2–4: Ch 1, sc in first st, dc in next st, [sc in next st, dc in next st] 4 times, turn.

Row 5: Ch 1, sc in first st, [dc in next st, sc in next st] 4 times, (dc, sc, dc) in last st, turn. *(6 sc, 6 dc)*

Row 6: Ch 1, sc in first st, dc in next st, [sc in next st, dc in next st] 5 times, turn.

Row 7: Ch 1, sc in first st, [dc in next st, sc in next st] 5 times, (dc, sc, dc) in last st, turn. *(7 sc, 7 dc)*

Row 8: Ch 1, sc in first st, dc in next st, [sc in next st, dc in next st] 6 times, fasten off.

Right Shoulder

Row 1 (RS): Ch 11, sc in 2nd ch from hook, dc in next ch, (sc in next ch, dc in next ch) across, turn. *(5 sc, 5 dc)*

Rows 2–8: Rep rows 2–8 of Left Shoulder. At end of last row, **do not fasten off**.

Bodice

Row 9: Ch 1, sc in first st, [dc in next st, sc in next st] 6 times, (dc, sc, dc) in next st, ch 11 [13, 15, 17], hold Left Shoulder with RS facing and row 8 at top, (dc, sc, dc) in first sc on row 8 of Left Shoulder, [sc in next st, dc in next st] 6 times, sc in last st, turn. *(32 sts, 11 [13, 15, 17] ch sts)*

Row 10: Ch 3 *(see Pattern Notes)*, sc in next st, [dc in next st, sc in next st] 7 times, dc in next ch, [sc in next ch, dc in next ch] 5 [6, 7, 8] times, [sc in next st, dc in next st] 8 times, turn. *(43 [45, 47, 49] sts)*

Row 11: Ch 1, sc in first st, *dc in next st, sc in next st, rep from * across to last st and turning ch-3, dc in last st, sc in 3rd ch of beg ch-3, turn.

Row 12: Ch 3, *sc in next st, dc in next st, rep from * across, turn.

Rows 13 & 14: Rep rows 11 and 12.

Row 15: Rep row 11.

Row 16: Ch 3, (sc, dc) in first st, *sc in next st, dc in next st, rep from * across to last st and beg ch-3, sc in last st, (dc, sc, dc) in 3rd ch of turning ch-3, turn. *(47 [49, 51, 53] sts)*

Row 17: Ch 1, sc in first st, *dc in next st, sc in next st, rep from * across to last st and beg ch-3, dc in last st, sc in 3rd ch of turning ch-3, turn.

Row 18: Ch 3, (sc, dc) in first st, *sc in next st, dc in next st, rep from * across to last st, (dc, sc, dc) in last st, turn. *(51 [53, 55, 57] sts)*

Rows 19–22: [Rep rows 17 and 18 alternately] twice. At end of last row, fasten off. *(59 [61, 63, 65] sts at end of last row)*

Rows 23–30 [23–32, 23–34, 23–36]: [Rep rows 11 and 12 alternately] 4 [5, 6, 7] times. At end of last row, fasten off.

Left Back

Row 1: Hold Left Shoulder with WS facing and beg ch at top, beg at neck edge, join with sl st in unused lp of first ch at right-hand edge, ch 1, sc in same lp, working in rem unused lp of beg ch, dc in next lp, [sc in next lp, dc in next lp] 4 times, turn. *(5 sc, 5 dc)*

Row 2: Ch 1, sc in first st, dc in next st, [sc in next st, dc in next st] 4 times, turn.

Row 3: Ch 1, (sc, dc, sc) in first st, dc in next st, [sc in next st, dc in next st] 4 times, turn. *(6 sc, 6 dc)*

Row 4: Ch 1, sc in first st, [dc in next st, sc in next st] 5 times, (dc, sc, dc) in last st. *(7 sc, 7 dc)*

Row 5: Ch 1, (sc, dc, sc) in first st, dc in next st, [sc in next st, dc in next st] 6 times, turn. *(8 sc, 8 dc)*

Row 6: Ch 1, sc in first st, dc in next st, [sc in next st, dc in next st] 7 times, insert hook in same sc as last sc made, yo, draw lp through, ch 1, yo, draw lp through 2 lps on hook—*inc made*, dc in last ch-1 sp made, *insert hook in same ch-1 sp as last dc made, yo, draw lp through, ch 1, yo, draw through 2 lps on hook—*inc made*, rep from * 0 [1, 2, 3] times, turn. *(20 [22, 24, 26] sts)*

Row 7: Ch 1, sc in first st, dc in next st, *sc in next st, dc in next st, rep from * across, turn.

Rows 8–15: Rep row 7.

Rows 16 & 17: Rep rows 3 and 4. *(24 [26, 28, 30] sts at end of last row)*

Row 18: Rep row 3. *(26 [28, 30, 32] sts)*

Rows 19–30 [19–32, 19–34, 19–36]: Rep row 7. At end of last row, fasten off.

Right Back

Row 1: Hold Right Shoulder with WS facing and beg ch at top, beg at armhole edge, join with sl st in first ch of row 1, **ch 3** *(see Pattern Notes)*, sc in next ch, [dc in next ch, sc in next ch] 4 times, turn. *(5 dc, 5 sc)*

Row 2: Ch 3, sc in next st, [dc in next st, sc in next st] 3 times, dc in next st, sc in 3rd ch of beg ch-3, turn.

Row 3: Ch 3, [sc in next st, dc in next st] 4 times, (sc, dc, sc) in last st, turn. *(6 dc, 6 sc)*

Row 4: Ch 3, (sc, dc) in first st, sc in next st, [dc in next st, sc in next st] 5 times, turn. *(7 dc, 7 sc)*

Row 5: Ch 3, [sc in next st, dc in next st] 6 times, (sc, dc, sc) in last st, turn. *(8 dc, 8 sc)*

Row 6: Ch 5 [6, 7, 8], sc in 4th ch from hook *(beg 3 sk chs count as dc)*, (dc, sc) in each of next 1 [2, 3, 4] chs, [dc in next st, sc in next st] 5 times, turn. *(20 [22, 24, 26] sts)*

Row 7: Ch 3, sc in next st, *dc in next st, sc in next st, rep from * across to last st and beg 3 sk chs, dc in next st, sc in 3rd ch of beg 3 sk chs, turn.

Rows 8–15: Rep row 7.

Row 16: Ch 3, sc in next st, *dc in next st, sc in next st, rep from * to last st, (sc, dc, sc) in last st, turn. *(22 [24, 26, 28] sts)*

Row 17: Ch 3, (sc, dc) in same st, sc in next st, (dc in next st, sc in next st) across, turn. *(24 [26, 28, 30] sts)*

Row 18: Rep row 16. *(26 [28, 30, 32] sts)*

Rows 19–30 [19–32, 19–34, 19–36]: Rep row 7. At end of last row, fasten off.

Buttonhole Placket

Row 1: With WS of Right Back facing, join with sl st in end of last row on Right Back, ch 1, sc in end of same row, work 30 [32, 35, 37] sc evenly spaced across side, turn. *(31 [33, 36, 38] sc)*

Row 2: Ch 1, sc in each sc across, turn.

Row 3: Ch 1, sc in each of first 3 [4, 3, 3] sc, *ch 2—*buttonhole made,* sk next 2 sc, sc in each of next 3 [3, 4, 4] sc, rep from * 4 times, sc in each of last 3 [4, 3, 4] sc, turn. *(5 buttonholes)*

Row 4: Ch 1, sc in each sc and ch across, fasten off.

Button Placket

Row 1: With RS of Back facing, join with sl st in end of last row 6 on Left Back, ch 1, sc in end of same row, work 30 [32, 35, 37] sc evenly spaced across side, turn. *(31 [33, 36, 38] sc)*

Rows 2–4: Ch 1, sc in each sc across, turn. At end of last row, fasten off.

Assembly

Sew underarm seams.

Skirt

Row 1: Join with sl st in end of row 4 on Buttonhole Placket at waist, ch 1, sc in end of same row, sc in each of next 3 rows, work 111 [117, 123, 129] sc evenly spaced around, skipping side seams and leaving ends of rows of Button Placket unworked, turn. *(115 [121, 127, 133] sc)*

Row 2: Ch 1, sc in each sc across, turn.

Row 3: Ch 1, sc in first sc, *ch 3, sk next 2 sc, **shell** *(see Special Stitch)* in next sc, ch 3, sk next 2 sc, sc in next sc, rep from * across, turn. *(19 [20, 21, 22] shells, 20 [21, 22, 23] sc)*

Row 4: Ch 3, 2 dc in first sc, ch 2, sk next ch-3 sp, sc in next ch-1 sp, [ch 3, sc in next ch-1 sp] 3 times, ch 2, sk next ch-3 sp, *(2 dc, ch 1, 2 dc) in next ch-1 sp, ch 2, sk next ch-3 sp, sc in next ch-1 sp, [ch 3, sc in next ch-1 sp] 3 times, ch 2, sk next ch-3 sp, rep from * across to last sc, 3 dc in last sc, turn.

Row 5: Ch 3, 2 dc in first dc, ch 2, sk next ch-2 sp, sc in next ch-3 sp, [ch 3, sc in next ch-3 sp] twice, ch 2, *(2 dc, ch 1, 2 dc) in next ch-1 sp, ch 2, sk next ch-2 sp, sc in next ch-3 sp, [ch 3, sc in next ch-3 sp] twice, ch 2, rep from * across to turning ch-3, 3 dc in 3rd ch of turning ch-3, turn.

Row 6: Ch 3, 2 dc in first dc, *sk next ch-2 sp, [ch 3, sc in next ch-3 sp] twice, ch 3, *(2 dc, ch 1, 2 dc) in next ch-1 sp, sk next ch-2 sp, [ch 3, sc in next ch-3 sp] twice, ch 3, rep from * across to turning ch-3, 3 dc in 3rd ch of turning ch-3, turn.

Row 7: Ch 1, sc in first dc, ch 3, sk next ch-3 sp, shell in next ch-3 sp, *ch 3, sc in next ch-1 sp, ch 3, sk next ch-3 sp, shell in next ch-3 sp, ch 3, rep from * across to turning ch-3, sc in 3rd ch of turning ch-3, turn.

Rows 8–23: [Rep rows 4–7 consecutively] 4 times.

Rows 24–26: Rep rows 4–6.

Row 27: Ch 3, 3 dc in first dc, sc in next ch-3 sp, 7 dc in next ch-3 lp, sc in next ch-3 sp, *7 dc in next ch-1 sp, sc in next ch-3 sp, 7 dc in next ch-3 sp, sc in next ch-3 sp, rep from * across to last sc, 3 dc in last sc, fasten off.

Finishing

Sew back Skirt seam across rows 9 through 27.

Collar

Row 1: Join with sl st in end of row 4 on Left Back at neck edge, ch 1, sc in same sp, work 54 sc evenly spaced around neck opening. *(55 sc)*

Row 2: Ch 1, sc in first sc, *ch 3, sk next 2 sc, shell in next sc, ch 3, sk next 2 sc, sc in next sc, rep from * across, turn. *(9 shells)*

Rows 3–5: Rep rows 4–6 of Skirt.

Row 6: Rep row 27 of Skirt, ending with 4 dc in last st. Fasten off.

Armhole Trim

Join with sl st in underarm seam on 1 armhole, ch 1, sc in same st, sc in each st and in end of each row around, join in first st, fasten off.

Rep on opposite armhole.

Finishing

Sew buttons on Left Back opposite buttonholes on Right Back. Sew optional hook and eye to top of neck opening and at waist. ∎

Vanilla Baby Dress

Skill Level
■ ■ ■ ▢ INTERMEDIATE

Finished Sizes
Instructions given fit size 12 months; changes for sizes 2, 3 and 4 are in [ ].

Materials
• Red Heart LusterSheen fine (sport) weight yarn (4 oz/335 yds/113g per skein):
   2 [3, 4, 5] skeins #0007 vanilla

• Size G/6/4.5mm crochet hook or size needed to obtain gauge
• Tapestry needle
• Sewing needle
• 2 yds ¼-inch-wide orange satin ribbon
• ½-inch shank buttons: 5
• 1 snap (optional)
• Matching thread

Gauge
16½ sc = 3¾ inches; 20 sc rows = 4 inches; [sc in next st, ch 2, (dc, picot, dc) in next ch-1 sp, ch 2] 3 times = 4 inches; 10 skirt pattern rows = 4 inches

Pattern Note
Weave in ends as work progresses.

Special Stitches
Picot: Ch 3, sl st in last st made.
Beginning shell (beg shell): Ch 3, 2 dc in indicated st.
Shell: (2 dc, ch 1, 2 dc) in indicated st.
End shell: 3 dc in indicated st.

Instructions

Front
Left Shoulder
Row 1 (RS): Starting at left shoulder, ch 8, sc in 2nd ch from hook, sc in each ch across, turn. *(7 sc)*
Rows 2–6: Ch 1, sc in each sc across, turn.
Row 7: Ch 1, 2 sc in first sc, sc in each sc across, turn. *(8 sc)*
Row 8: Ch 1, sc in each sc across, turn.
Row 9: Ch 1, 2 sc in first sc, sc in each sc across, turn. *(9 sc)*

Row 10: Ch 1, sc in each sc across, turn.

Rows 11 & 12 [11 & 12, 11 & 12, 11–14]: [Rep rows 9 and 10 alternately] once [once, once, twice]. At end of last row, fasten off. (10 [10, 10, 11] sc at end of last row)

Right Shoulder

Row 1 (RS): Ch 8, sc in 2nd ch from hook, sc in each ch across, turn. (7 sc)

Rows 2–6: Ch 1, sc in each sc across, turn.

Row 7: Ch 1, sc in each sc across to last sc, 2 sc in last sc, turn. (8 sc)

Row 8: Ch 1, sc in each sc across, turn.

Row 9: Ch 1, 2 sc in first sc, sc in each sc across, turn. (9 sc)

Row 10: Ch 1, sc in each sc across, turn.

Rows 11 & 12 [11 & 12, 11 & 12, 11–14]: [Rep rows 9 and 10 alternately] once [once, once, twice]. (10 [10, 10, 11] sc at end of last row)

Bodice

Row 13 [13, 13, 15]: Ch 1, sc in each st across to last sc, 2 sc in last st, ch 13 [15, 17, 19], join with sc in last st on wrong side of row 11 on Left shoulder, sc in same st, sc in each st across, turn. (22 [22, 22, 24] sc, 13 [15, 17, 19] ch sts)

Row 14 [14, 14, 16]: Ch 1, sc in each st and ch across, turn. (35 [37, 39, 43] sc)

Rows 15–20 [15–20, 15–20, 16–22]: Ch 1, sc in each st across, turn.

Rows 21–24 [21–24, 21–26, 23–28]: Ch 1, 2 sc in first st, sc in each st across to last sc, 2 sc in last sc, turn. At end of last row, fasten off. (43 [45, 51, 55] sc at end of last row)

Back
Right Shoulder

Row 1 (WS): Hold Bodice with WS facing, join with sl st in unused lp of first ch of beg ch of Right Shoulder, ch 1, sc in same lp, working in rem unused lps of beg ch, sc in each lp across, turn. (7 sc)

Rows 2–5: Ch 1, sc in each sc across, turn.

Row 6: Ch 1, 2 sc in first sc, sc in each sc across, turn. (8 sc)

Row 7: Ch 1, sc in each sc across, turn.

Row 8: Ch 1, 2 sc in first sc, sc in each sc across, turn. (9 sc)

Rows 9 & 10 [9 & 10, 9 & 10, 9–12]: [Rep rows 7 and 8 alternately] once [once, once, twice]. (10 [10, 10, 11] sc at end of last row)

Row 11 [11, 11, 13]: Ch 1, sc in each st across to last sc, 2 sc in last sc, turn. (11 [11, 11, 12] sc)

Row 12 [12, 12, 14]: Ch 7 [9, 11, 11], sc in 2nd ch from hook, sc in each ch and st across, turn. (17 [19, 21, 22] sc)

Rows 13–20 [13–20, 13–22, 15–24]: Rep row 2.

Row 21 [21, 23, 25]: Rep row 6. (18 [20, 22, 23] sc)

Row 22 [22, 24, 26]: Rep row 11. (19 [21, 23, 24] sc)

Row 23 [23, 25, 27]: Rep row 6. (20 [22, 24, 25] sc)

Row 24 [24, 26, 28]: Rep row 11. At end of row, fasten off. (21 [23, 25, 26] sc)

Left Shoulder

Row 1: Hold Bodice with WS facing, join in unused lp of first ch of beg ch of Left Shoulder, ch 1, sc in same lp, working in rem unused lps of beg ch, sc in each lp across, turn. (7 sc)

Rows 2–5: Ch 1, sc in each sc across, turn.

Row 6: Ch 1, sc in each sc across to last sc, 2 sc in last sc, turn. (8 sc)

Row 7: Ch 1, sc in each sc across, turn.

Row 8: Ch 1, 2 sc in first sc, sc in each sc across, turn. (9 sc)

Rows 9 & 10 [9 & 10, 9 & 10, 9–12]: [Rep rows 7 and 8 alternately] once [once, once, twice]. (10 [10, 10, 11] sc at end of last row)

Row 11 [11, 11, 13]: Ch 1, 2 sc in first sc, sc in each sc across, turn. (11 [11, 11, 12] sc)

Row 12 [12, 12, 14]: Ch 1, sc in each sc across, insert hook in same sc as last sc made, yo, draw lp through, ch 1, yo, draw lp through 2 lps on hook—inc made, *insert hook in last ch-1 sp made, yo, draw lp through, ch 1, yo, draw through 2 lps on hook—inc made, rep from * 4 [6, 8, 8] times, turn. (17 [19, 21, 22] sc)

Rows 13–20 [13–20, 13–22, 15–24]: Rep row 2.

Row 21 [21, 23, 25]: Rep row 6. (18 [20, 22, 23] sc)

Row 22 [22, 24, 26]: Rep row 11. (19 [21, 23, 24] sc)

Row 23 [23, 25, 27]: Rep row 6. (20 [22, 24, 25] sc)

Row 24 [24, 26, 28]: Rep row 11. At end of row, fasten off. (21 [23, 25, 26] sc)

Empire Waist Section

Row 1: Hold Back with RS facing and last row of Right Shoulder at top, join with sl st in first sc on last row of Right Shoulder, ch 1, sc in same st, sc in each st across, working across Front, sc in each st across last row of Front, working across Left Shoulder on Back, sc in each st across last row of Left Shoulder, turn. (85 [91, 101, 107] sc)

Row 2: Ch 4 (counts as a dc and ch-1 sp), sk next sc, dc in next sc, *ch 1, sk next sc, dc in next sc, rep from * across, turn. (43 [46, 51, 54] dc, 42 [45, 50, 53] ch-1 sps)

Row 3: Ch 1, sc in each st and ch sp across to beg ch-4 of row 2, sc in each of next 2 chs of beg ch-4, **do not turn.** (85 [91, 101, 107] sc)

Left Back Placket

Row 1: Ch 1, working across next side in ends of rows, sc in end of row 3, 2 sc in end of next row, sc in end of each of next 15 [15, 15, 17] rows, turn. (18 [18, 18, 20] sc)

Row 2: Ch 1, sc in each sc across, turn.

Row 3: Ch 1, sc in each of first 2 [2, 2, 3] sc, [ch 2—*buttonhole made*, sk next 2 sc, sc in each of next 2 sc] 4 times, sc in each of next 0 [0, 0, 2] sc, turn. *(10 [10, 10, 13] sc, 4 buttonholes)*

Row 4: Ch 1, sc in each sc and in each ch across, fasten off. *(18 [18, 18, 20] sc)*

Skirt

Row 1 (WS): Hold Bodice with WS facing, join in end of row 4 on Left Back Placket, ch 1, sc in same sp, ch 2, (dc, **picot**—*see Special Stitches*, dc) in end of next row, ch 2, sc in end of next row, ch 2, (dc, picot, dc) in end of next row, *ch 2, sc in next sc, ch 2, (dc, picot, dc) in next sc, rep from * across to last st, ch 2, sc in last st, turn. *(44 [47, 52, 55] picot, 45 [48, 53, 56] sc)*

Row 2 (RS): Beg shell *(see Special Stitches)* in first sc, *ch 1, **shell** *(see Special Stitches)* in next sc, rep from * across to last sc, ch 1, **end shell** *(see Special Stitches)* in last sc, turn. *(43 [46, 51, 54] shells, 44 [47, 52, 55] ch sts, 1 beg shell, 1 end shell)*

Row 3: Ch 1, sc in first st, ch 3, (dc, picot, dc) in next ch-1 sp, ch 3, *sc in ch-1 sp of next shell, ch 3, (dc, picot, dc) in next ch-1 sp, ch 3,

rep from * across to beg ch-3, sc in 3rd ch of beg ch-3, turn.

Row 4: Beg shell in first sc, *ch 1, shell in next sc, rep from * across to last sc, end shell in last sc, turn.

Rows 5–22: [Rep rows 3 and 4 alternately] 9 times.

Row 23: Rep row 3. At end of row, fasten off.

Assembly

Sew back seam beg at row 23 and ending at row 8.

Trims

Left Back Placket & Neck Trim

Row 1 (RS): Hold Bodice with RS facing, join with sl st in first sc on row 4 of Left Back Placket, ch 1, sc in same sc, sc in each sc across to last sc, (sc, ch 1, sc) in last sc—*corner made*, working in ends of rows across placket, sc in row, working around neck edge in ends of rows and in sc, sc evenly spaced to row 12 [12, 12, 14] of Back Right Shoulder, (sc, ch 1, sc) in end of row—*corner made*, working in ends of rows across next side of same shoulder, sc in each row to row 2 of Empire Waist Section, 2 sc in row 2, sc in row 1, fasten off.

Row 2: Join with sl st in first st of last row, ch 1, *(sc, picot) in next st, ch 1, sk next st, rep from * across to last 2 sts before next

corner on Right Back, (sc, picot) twice in ch-1 sp of corner, sc in each sc across to ch-1 sp of next corner, sc in ch-1 sp, sc in next sc, working across next side, sc in each sc across, turn.

Row 3: Ch 1, sc in each sc across Placket, fasten off, leaving rem sts unworked.

Armhole Trim

Rnd 1: Hold 1 armhole with RS facing, join with sl st in first st at bottom of underarm, ch 1, sc evenly spaced around, join in first sc, fasten off.

Rnd 2: Join with sl st in first sc of rnd 1, ch 1, (sc, picot) in same sc, ch 1, sk next sc, *(sc, picot) in next sc, ch 1, sk next sc, rep from * around, join in first sc, fasten off.

Rep in rem armhole.

Finishing

Sew Buttons to Placket opposite buttonholes. Cut ribbon in half. Sew end of 1 length to WS of Placket, at row 2 of Empire Waist Section. Weave through ch-1 sps around to center Front. With rem length, rep on opposite Placket and weave in same row around to center front. Tie in bow. Sew optional snap to top of back opening and to end of Placket at waist back opening. ∎

General Information

Standard Yarn Weight System
Categories of yarn, gauge ranges, and recommended hook sizes

Yarn Weight Symbol & Category Names	1 SUPER FINE	2 FINE	3 LIGHT	4 MEDIUM	5 BULKY	6 SUPER BULKY
Type of Yarns in Category	Sock, Fingering, Baby	Sport, Baby	DK, Light Worsted	Worsted, Afghan, Aran	Chunky, Craft, Rug	Bulky, Roving
Crochet Gauge* Ranges in Single Crochet to 4 inch	21–32 sts	16–20 sts	12–17 sts	11–14 sts	8–11 sts	5–9 sts
Recommended Hook in Metric Size Range	2.25–3.25mm	3.5–4.5mm	4.5–5.5mm	5.5–6.5mm	6.5–9mm	9mm and larger
Recommended Hook U.S. Size Range	B/1–E/4	E/4–7	7–I/9	I/9–K/10½	K/10½–M/13	M/13 and larger

* GUIDELINES ONLY: The above reflect the most commonly used gauges and hook sizes for specific yarn categories.

Skill Levels

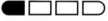

BEGINNER
Beginner projects for first-time crocheters using basic stitches. Minimal shaping.

EASY
Easy projects using basic stitches, repetitive stitch patterns, simple color changes and simple shaping and finishing.

INTERMEDIATE
Intermediate projects with a variety of stitches, mid-level shaping and finishing.

EXPERIENCED
Experienced projects using advanced techniques and stitches, detailed shaping and refined finishing.

How to Check Gauge

A correct stitch-gauge is very important. Please take the time to work a stitch-gauge swatch about 4 x 4 inches. Measure the swatch. If the number of stitches and rows is fewer than indicated under "Gauge" in the pattern, your hook is too large. Try another swatch with a smaller size hook. If the number of stitches and rows is more than indicated under "Gauge" in the pattern, your hook is too small. Try another swatch with a larger size hook.

Symbols

* An asterisk (or double asterisk **) is used to mark the beginning of a portion of instructions to be worked more than once; thus, "rep from * twice more" means after working the instructions once, repeat the instructions following the asterisk twice more (3 times in all).

[] Brackets are used to enclose instructions that should be worked the exact number of times specified immediately following the brackets, such as "[2 sc in next dc, sc in next dc] twice."

[] Brackets and () parentheses are used to provide additional information to clarify instructions.

Stitch Guide

For more complete information, visit **AnniesAttic.com**

Abbreviations

beg	begin/beginning
bpdc	back post double crochet
bpsc	back post single crochet
bptr	back post treble crochet
CC	contrasting color
ch	chain stitch
ch-	refers to chain or space previously made (i.e., ch-1 space)
ch sp	chain space
cl	cluster
cm	centimeter(s)
dc	double crochet
dec	decrease/decreases/decreasing
dtr	double treble crochet
fpdc	front post double crochet
fpsc	front post single crochet
fptr	front post treble crochet
g	gram(s)
hdc	half double crochet
inc	increase/increases/increasing
lp(s)	loop(s)
MC	main color
mm	millimeter(s)
oz	ounce(s)
pc	popcorn
rem	remain/remaining
rep	repeat(s)
rnd(s)	round(s)
RS	right side
sc	single crochet
sk	skip(ped)
sl st	slip stitch
sp(s)	space(s)
st(s)	stitch(es)
tog	together
tr	treble crochet
trtr	triple treble crochet
WS	wrong side
yd(s)	yard(s)
yo	yarn over

Chain—ch: Yo, pull through lp on hook.

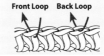

Slip stitch—sl st: Insert hook in st, pull through both lps on hook.

Single crochet—sc: Insert hook in st, yo, pull through st, yo, pull through both lps on hook.

Front post stitch—fp: Back post stitch—bp: When working post st, insert hook from right to left around post st on previous row.

Back Front

Front loop—front lp Back loop— back lp

Front Loop   Back Loop

Half double crochet—hdc: Yo, insert hook in st, yo, pull through st, yo, pull through all 3 lps on hook.

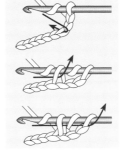

Double crochet—dc: Yo, insert hook in st, yo, pull through st, [yo, pull through 2 lps] twice.

Change colors: Drop first color; with 2nd color, pull through last 2 lps of st.

Treble crochet—tr: Yo twice, insert hook in st, yo, pull through st, [yo, pull through 2 lps] 3 times.

Double treble crochet—dtr: Yo 3 times, insert hook in st, yo, pull through st, [yo, pull through 2 lps], 4 times.

Single crochet decrease (sc dec): (Insert hook, yo, draw lp through) in each of the sts indicated, yo, draw through all lps on hook.

Example of 2-sc dec

Half double crochet decrease (hdc dec): (Yo, insert hook, yo, draw lp through) in each of the sts indicated, yo, draw through all lps on hook.

Example of 2-hdc dec

Double crochet decrease (dc dec): (Yo, insert hook, yo, draw loop through, draw through 2 lps on hook) in each of the sts indicated, yo, draw through all lps on hook.

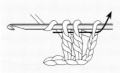

Example of 2-dc dec

Treble crochet decrease (tr dec): Holding back last lp of each st, tr in each of the sts indicated, yo, pull through all lps on hook.

US		UK
sl st (slip stitch)	=	sc (single crochet)
sc (single crochet)	=	dc (double crochet)
hdc (half double crochet)	=	htr (half treble crochet)
dc (double crochet)	=	tr (treble crochet)
tr (treble crochet)	=	dtr (double treble crochet)
dtr (double treble crochet)	=	ttr (triple treble crochet)
skip	=	miss

Inches Into Millimeters & Centimeters

All measurements are rounded off slightly.

inches	mm	cm	inches	cm	inches	cm	inches	cm
⅛	3	0.3	5	12.5	21	53.5	38	96.5
¼	6	0.6	5½	14	22	56.0	39	99.0
⅜	10	1.0	6	15.0	23	58.5	40	101.5
½	13	1.3	7	18.0	24	61.0	41	104.0
⅝	15	1.5	8	20.5	25	63.5	42	106.5
¾	20	2.0	9	23.0	26	66.0	43	109.0
⅞	22	2.2	10	25.5	27	68.5	44	112.0
1	25	2.5	11	28.0	28	71.0	45	114.5
1¼	32	3.8	12	30.5	29	73.5	46	117.0
1½	38	3.8	13	33.0	30	76.0	47	119.5
1¾	45	4.5	14	35.5	31	79.0	48	122.0
2	50	5.0	15	38.0	32	81.5	49	124.5
2½	65	6.5	16	40.5	33	84.0	50	127.0
3	75	7.5	17	43.0	34	86.5		
3½	90	9.0	18	46.0	35	89.0		
4	100	10.0	19	48.5	36	91.5		
4½	115	11.5	20	51.0	37	94.0		

Crochet Hooks Conversion Chart

U.S.	1/B	2/C	3/D	4/E	5/F	6/G	8/H	9/I	10/J	10½/K	N
Continental-mm	2.25	2.75	3.25	3.5	3.75	4.25	5	5.5	6	6.5	9.0

American School of Needlework ®
excellence in instruction

TOLL-FREE ORDER LINE or to request a free catalog (800) 582-6643
Customer Service (800) 282-6643, **Fax** (800) 882-6643

Visit DRGnetwork.com.

We have made every effort to ensure the accuracy and completeness of these instructions.
We cannot, however, be responsible for human error, typographical mistakes or variations in individual work.

ISBN: 978-1-59012-214-3   All rights reserved.   Printed in USA   1 2 3 4 5 6 7 8 9